DATE DUE			

Mozart

YOUNG MUSIC GENIUS

Mozart
YOUNG MUSIC GENIUS

by Francene Sabin
illustrated by Yoshi Miyake

Troll Associates

Library of Congress Cataloging-in-Publication Data

Sabin, Francene.
    Mozart, young music genius / by Francene Sabin; illustrated by
Yoshi Miyake.
        p.   cm.
    Summary: A brief biography of Mozart, emphasizing the first six
years of his musically productive life.
    ISBN 0-8167-1773-7 (lib. bdg.)   ISBN 0-8167-1774-5 (pbk.)
    1. Mozart, Wolfgang Amadeus, 1756-1791—Juvenile literature.
2. Composers—Austria—Biography—Juvenile literature. [1. Mozart,
Wolfgang Amadeus, 1756-1791—Childhood and youth. 2. Composers.]
I. Miyake, Yoshi, ill. II. Title.
ML3930.M9S18 1990
[92]—dc20   89-33980

Printed in the United States of America.
10   9   8   7   6   5   4   3   2   1

Mozart

YOUNG MUSIC GENIUS

Candles blazed, lighting the huge, handsome room. Finely dressed ladies and gentlemen sat on delicate chairs with satin seats. They spoke softly as they waited for the musical performance to begin. At one end of the room stood a harpsichord. This instrument, an early form of the piano, was made of beautifully carved wood. In front of the instrument's keyboard stood a chair with two cushions on it.

The ladies and gentlemen stopped talking as a little boy entered the room. The youngster wore a silk coat and knee breeches. His stockings were white and his black shoes had silver buckles. His shirt had lace ruffles at the cuffs and collar. And topping all this was a powdered white wig set firmly on his head. The five-year-old looked exactly like a tiny version of the adult men in the room.

Smiling brightly, the boy bowed to his audience and climbed onto the cushioned chair. He sat still for a moment, staring at the keyboard. Then he began to play. His small fingers flew over the keys. Lovely sounds flowed like a silver stream from the instrument. It was amazing that so young a child could play music so well.

When the boy finished playing, the audience applauded and asked for more. The young musician was happy to play on. He was glad that they liked his performance. And he loved to play music. As long as there was an audience that enjoyed his music, he could play all night.

Leopold Mozart, the boy's father, stood at the back of the room. He was proud of little Wolfgang. The child was a genius. Mr. Mozart knew it, and with each concert more people would know it. This was important to the Mozart family. As the boy's fame grew, so would the payment he would receive for concerts. That meant a great deal, because Mr. Mozart hoped that Wolfgang's earnings would help to increase the family's income.

Mr. Mozart was a well-respected violinist and music teacher. He was employed by Count Schrattenbach in the city of Salzburg, Austria. The count ruled the Court of Salzburg, which employed twenty-two musicians, an orchestra leader, and his assistant. The group performed at church services, dinners, balls, and other official functions. Mr. Mozart was the leader's assistant. His goal had always been to become the orchestra's leader. It was the only musical position at the court that paid enough to support a family well.

Leopold Mozart was a talented violinist as well as composer. His book *The Violin School* was a standard work in the musical world. But he was never appointed leader of the court orchestra, and he never earned much money. Today he is best remembered as the teacher and business manager of his gifted children.

Leopold and his wife, Anna Maria, had seven children. But only two of them lived past infancy.

They were Maria Anna, called Nannerl, who was
born on July 30, 1751, and Wolfgang Amadeus,
who was born on January 27, 1756. Nannerl
began taking music lessons from Papa Mozart
when she was about four years old. She learned
to play the harpsichord, the clavier (another early
form of the piano), and the piano. But her special
talent was singing. Nannerl had a sweet voice and
a charming personality that delighted listeners.

When he was a baby, Wolfgang would lie in his
cradle and listen to Nannerl's music lessons. He
also listened quietly while Papa Mozart practiced
the violin. As the boy grew a bit older, it was clear
that he enjoyed music. Papa Mozart was thrilled
at his little son's interest in music, but he did not
want to start teaching him too soon.

Wolfgang couldn't wait for regular lessons. When he was three years old, he began to teach himself to play the clavier. He would climb up on the chair in front of the instrument and pick out tunes that he had heard his father and sister play. Wolfgang was so small that he could not reach the keys while sitting. So he knelt on the seat. For hours he would try to play chords and songs with his tiny hands.

Experimenting with the clavier was fun, but it was not enough for Wolfgang. He wanted to learn to read music and to play instruments properly. Even though it annoyed Nannerl, Wolfgang started to interrupt her lessons with Papa.

Finally, Mr. Mozart told his son, "I will give you lessons in music. But there are two things you must do. One, you must practice every day and learn each lesson perfectly before we go on to the next one. Two, you must let Nannerl have her lessons to herself. She will not disturb you, and you will not disturb her. Agreed?"

Little Wolfgang's eyes shone. This is what he had been waiting for. The next day the lessons began. Now four years old, Wolfgang immediately showed his talent. Many children don't like to practice their music lessons for more than an hour a day. Wolfgang never wanted to stop practicing.

Years later, Nannerl wrote, "As soon as Wolfgang began to give himself to music, all his senses were as good as dead to other activities.

Even his pranks and games with toys had to be
done to music if he was going to enjoy them. When
he and I carried toys for a game from one room
to another, whichever of us was empty-handed had
to sing and play a march on the fiddle."

15

At about this same time, Wolfgang invented a bedtime game. Every night, he would sing a little melody he had thought up during the day. Papa Mozart would have to listen carefully and make up a harmony to sing with Wolfgang's new tune. Father and son would sing together, harmonizing like two musical instruments. Then, after the last note of their vocal duet had faded, there was a goodnight hug and kiss.

For the boy, the singing ritual was a wonderful game. It was as relaxing as a bedtime story, and it was fun for Papa Mozart too. But Wolfgang saw more in it than just a bedtime game. Each day, the boy's tunes became more interesting, more musically developed. And the harmonizing was teaching Wolfgang how music blended sounds.

Papa Mozart knew Wolfgang was making great progress in music. But even he was not fully aware of his son's genius—until about a year later.

It happened on the day two fellow musicians from the court orchestra came over to practice a composition Leopold had written for harpsichord and two violins. As the three men were setting up their music stands to practice, five-year-old Wolfgang walked into the room. He was holding a half-sized violin. "Papa," he said, "please let me play the second-violin part."

Mr. Mozart smiled, but shook his head. Wolfgang asked again. Patiently, Papa Mozart told the youngster, "First, you must take violin lessons. Then, when you play the instrument properly, we will make music together."

Wolfgang began to cry. "Please, Papa. Let me try."

Johann Schachtner, the second violinist, said, "Leopold, let the boy play along with me. It can do no harm."

Mr. Mozart agreed, but told Wolfgang, "You must play so softly that we can't hear you, or you will have to leave."

The musicians began to play. Mr. Schachtner
played for a while, then he stopped and put down
his violin. The boy played on. It was magic.
Leopold, hearing the beauty of his son's second-
violin part and seeing that Mr. Schachtner was
no longer playing, was stunned. It was a moment
of joy and wonder, and tears came to his eyes.

The next day, Wolfgang began formal violin lessons with his father. The boy had taught himself a great deal, but there was still much to learn. As he had with the keyboard instruments, the youngster was happy to practice the violin for hours. And his progress was amazing. He was a quick learner, but there was something else that made his progress especially fast. Wolfgang had an ability called absolute pitch. It is a kind of musical memory that makes it possible for a person to be able to identify and recall perfectly the way a note should sound.

Wolfgang's musical memory was especially sharp. Once, after a concert given by the court orchestra, Wolfgang surprised Mr. Schachtner by saying, "Your violin is tuned half a quarter-tone lower than mine."

Several musicians heard the remark and laughed. Schachtner, who knew the child's talent, nodded. "Very likely," he said.

The other musicians grinned at Schachtner. "You must be mad," one of them said, "taking a five-year-old boy seriously."

Schachtner simply replied, "Are you willing to bet on that?" The other musician agreed, and the two of them walked home with Wolfgang and Mr. Mozart. There, Mr. Schachtner played a series of tones called a scale on his own violin. Next, he played the same scale on the boy's violin. Just as Wolfgang had said, the difference in tone was plainly heard. Schachtner turned and smiled at the musician who had doubted Wolfgang's musical ear. Without a word, the man bowed to the two adults, then lifted little Wolfgang and kissed him on each cheek.

Wolfgang's absolute pitch was of great importance to him in many ways. It not only helped him to recognize and play music, but it also helped him to compose music. The boy was interested in writing music just as his beloved father did. And Wolfgang's first musical works, composed when he was five years old, were two short pieces for the clavier.

The music came quickly to the youngster's mind. But he could not write down all the notes he heard in his head. That was because he was just starting to learn to write—both musical marks and alphabet letters. So the boy wrote down the notes as well as he could, and played the rest of them. Papa Mozart would then write down what Wolfgang played. Leopold handed the sheets of music to his son, and they both smiled proudly.

A few months later, Mr. Mozart, accompanied by Johann Schachtner, came home from orchestra rehearsal. They found Wolfgang busy at Mr. Mozart's writing desk. Ink stains spattered the desk, the boy's hands and clothes, and the sheets of music papers spread over the room. "What are you writing?" Papa Mozart asked.

"A concerto for clavier and orchestra," Wolfgang said happily. A concerto is a musical composition for an orchestra and usually one solo instrument.

Mr. Mozart looked at what his son had written. After studying it for a moment, he handed the sheets of music to Schachtner. The concerto wasn't easy to read, because of all the smudges and ink blots covering the pages. But it soon became clear to both men that it was a very advanced piece of work.

"Wolfgang, this is very beautiful," Leopold Mozart said. "But I think it cannot be played. It is just too difficult."

"I know, Papa," the boy protested. "It is *supposed* to be difficult. It is a concerto, and a concerto must not be too easy. It must be practiced over and over until it is played right."

The boy then sat down at the clavier and tried to play his own music for the first time. But it was much harder to play than the way it had sounded in his head. He tried to play it again and again, but the results were the same. Wolfgang stared at the music he had written and frowned. After a few moments, he sighed and smiled sadly. Wolfgang realized he had been wrong to think that good music had to be almost impossible to perform. It was an important lesson for the young genius. From that day on, he never forgot that music comes alive only when it is played or sung. If nobody can perform the music, it is no better than inkblots on a piece of paper.

Mozart, as an adult composer, often wrote music that was technically demanding to perform. But some of his music was very easy to play or sing. Still, easy or hard, his music was always extraordinary and always written with the performer in mind. If he wrote violin music, for example, he made sure that the notes were within the range of a violin. And, of course, he made sure it would be possible for a violinist to play the notes.

In the same way, Mozart's operas were perfectly suited to the human voice. His songs never called for a high voice to sing notes that were too low for that voice. And he always remembered to write vocal music that let the singers breathe. He knew that a voice sounds harsh and forced if the singer must sing too many notes in a row without taking a breath. Mozart wanted the songs of his operas to sound smooth and beautiful. He succeeded so well that his operas are considered to be among the most beautiful ever written.

In the early part of 1762, when Wolfgang was six years old, he was taken on his first musical tour. Mr. Mozart, Nannerl, and Wolfgang went to the city of Munich for a three-week stay. It was carnival time in Munich, a time filled with concerts, dances, parties, firework displays, operas, and street fairs. Leopold wanted the children to have fun, but he had another, more important reason for the trip to Munich. He felt this was the perfect moment for the children to launch their music careers beyond Salzburg.

There were no public concerts for which people could buy tickets to attend, as there are today. Concerts were given to entertain rich and noble families. The musicians played in the drawing rooms of castles and mansions. The rich and noble families, called patrons, paid the composers for writing music. They also paid the musicians for playing that music. But the payment depended on the feelings and the generosity of the patron.

For example, a count might tell a composer to write an opera to be performed for a special occasion. The composer had no idea of what the payment would be. It might be money, an expensive watch, or a suit of fine clothing. However, if a patron was not pleased with the opera, there might be no payment at all. It was a risky business, but it was the only way a composer could get his or her music played.

When musicians wanted to perform in a city, they had to give their first concert for the highest-ranking noble or royal person of that city. To do this, the musician had to be invited by that person. Then, if the concert proved successful, other wealthy people of the city invited the musicians to perform at their homes.

In Munich, the ranking noble was called the Elector of Bavaria. Leopold Mozart had a letter of introduction to the elector and was able to arrange an invitation for his children to perform. The concert was a great success. Nannerl sang very well, but it was Wolfgang who was a sensation. Not only was he just six years old, but he was also small for his age—not much bigger than most three- or four-year-olds. He played the clavier and the violin. Again and again, the audience's applause filled the grand ballroom. They did not want the little boy to stop playing. And he didn't want to stop.

For Wolfgang's final number, a clever routine was used. A long strip of cloth was hung just above the clavier's keyboard. The cloth blocked Wolfgang's view of the keyboard, although he still had enough room to get his hands underneath to play. With the cloth in place, Mr. Mozart then asked the elector to choose a piece of music that everyone knew. And Wolfgang played the music chosen. After he played the piece through once, the boy genius played it in different ways, called variations. These thrilled the audience because he was composing the variations in his head as he played. And all of this was done with Wolfgang unable to see his hands or the keyboard underneath the cloth. He had to know the instrument by touch and the music by ear.

The Mozarts were a great success in Munich.
They were in constant demand to perform at
palaces and mansions. In their three-week stay,
Wolfgang and his sister earned a large sum of
money and other rewards. Mr. Mozart was very
pleased, and he began to make plans for longer
tours throughout Europe.

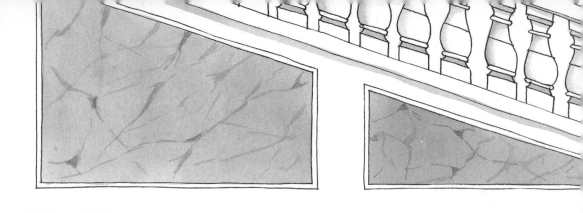

That September, the Mozarts went to Vienna, the capital of Austria. There, they performed for Empress Maria Theresa and her court. After the concert, which delighted the audience, the empress's children showed Wolfgang and Nannerl all the rooms of the palace. While walking through one of the large rooms, Wolfgang slipped on the polished marble floor. He fell with a *thump*! One of the princesses, the pretty Marie Antoinette, rushed to help him. Six-year-old Wolfgang thanked the little princess for her kindness and asked her to marry him. Marie Antoinette, who was only two months older than the boy, blushed and giggled. Years later, when Marie Antoinette was queen of France, Mozart enjoyed telling the story of his brief romance with "Her Majesty."

From Vienna, the Mozarts traveled by horse-drawn coach to the great cities of Germany, where they put on many concerts. Wolfgang played brilliantly, but the concert tour had to be ended when the young musician became ill. Mr. Mozart thought that the cause was overwork and that a few months of rest were all Wolfgang needed.

We now know that Wolfgang Mozart suffered from a serious kidney disease. It was the reason for his extreme shortness and frail health. Throughout his life Wolfgang was often sick.

After six months of rest, following little Wolfgang's first bout with kidney disease, the family set out on a grand tour of Europe. For three and a half years they traveled from city to city, country to country. Before they were done, the Mozarts had performed for the royalty of England, France, Belgium, and the Netherlands, as well as for the ruling families of Switzerland and Germany.

This tour and the many tours that followed set the pattern Wolfgang would follow for all his life. He played concerts during the afternoon and early evening. He composed music during the morning and at night, sometimes working all night through. So long as Wolfgang was a youngster, his father handled all the details of day-to-day living. The boy's whole life was music. Unfortunately, he never learned to take care of himself. Even when he was grown up, married, and the father of two sons, Mozart had no idea of how to manage his career.

Sometimes Mozart earned a great deal of money, but he spent it as quickly as he earned it. He bought fine clothes, gave lavish parties, rented expensive places to live, and hired many servants. Then, when there was no money, he was forced to sell his possessions and to compose more music at a feverish pace.

On December 5, 1791, Wolfgang died following
another illness. He was just thirty-five years old.
Stories circulated that Wolfgang had been
poisoned by a rival composer who was jealous of
him. But doctors now agree that the only "poison"
in Mozart's body was created by his damaged
kidneys, from which he suffered all his life.

The music Wolfgang Amadeus Mozart composed
in the thirty-five years of his life is extraordinary
both in output and in beauty. It includes fifteen

masses to be sung at church services, and more than a dozen shorter religious compositions. Among his twenty-two operas are some of the finest ever written, such as *The Marriage of Figaro, The Magic Flute,* and *Don Giovanni.* Mozart wrote forty-eight symphonies, six full-length and three shorter concertos for violin, and twenty-five piano concertos. He also wrote sonatas (musical compositions for one or two instruments) and concertos for flute, harp, viola, clarinet, bassoon, and many other instruments.

47

Still, Mozart's music was not often played after his death. That is because the composer could rarely afford to have his music printed. So other musicians had no sheet music to play from. It was almost a century later that Mozart's musical outpourings were catalogued and published. And since then, millions of music lovers have listened to the glorious creations of the boy genius of Salzburg.